CHARACTER TRAILS

Learning to Walk in Paths of Righteousness

Character Trails: Learning to Walk in Paths of Righteousness

Copyright © 2011 by Marilyn Boyer

ALL RIGHTS RESERVED

Everyday Life stories by Laura Boyer
History and Bible stories by Devin Dahl

Photography by Kate Boyer Brown, Kelley Boyer, and Laura Boyer

Graphics and layout design by Mary Ann Edman

First printing November, 2011
Second printing March, 2014
Third printing April, 2015

ISBN 978-0-9777685-3-0

Published by The Learning Parent
2430 Sunnymeade Road
Rustburg, VA 24588
www.thelearningparent.com

Proudly printed in the United States of America by Jostens

CHARACTER TRAILS

Learning to Walk in Paths of Righteousness

by Marilyn Boyer

RUSTBURG, VIRGINIA

How to Use Character Trails

Character Trails is the second book in our *Character Concepts Curriculum.* It is suggested for use with kindergarteners through third graders. The book covers 12 character qualities which are presented in such a way that children of this age group can grasp the meaning.

Each character quality is studied through the use of three stories, one featuring a hero from Scripture, one featuring an inspiring hero from history, and one following the Boyer cousins as they learn to make wise decisions in everyday life. If you choose to use this book as a year's worth of character lessons, you can read one story each week, answer one of the three questions at the end of the chapter and implement one of the practical projects (which is located at the end of each chapter as well) each week as well. The application questions and practical projects are designed to guide your child in internalizing what they learn and applying it to everyday life.

Available online are Bible coloring pages, one for each Bible story in the book, that you can print to allow your child to color while you are reading the Bible story to him/her. (Just go to our website www.thelearningparent.com and place *Character Trails Coloring Pages* in your cart. Proceed to the checkout, use code COLOR and they will be free.) Our children would then like hanging the finished product on the refrigerator which is a reminder all week long of the character quality you are studying. Remember to praise your child as he learns to implement the quality in his everyday life, and gently guide him as opportunities arise to practice what he is learning.

Also available from The Learning Parent are *Character Trails* flashcards which are used to help cement the Scripture verses in your child's mind. There is one verse to learn for each character quality covered. We drill the verse each day for a few minutes and at the end of three weeks they should be able to easily quote the verse. Review previously learned verses once or twice a week as well. As God's Word never returns void, you will begin to see your child learn to apply God's Word to his life as time goes on and he begins to "own" the Bible verses he has learned.

You may find your child wants to have the stories read to him many times. That is fine. Don't feel like you just read it once and then have to wait until the following week to read any more. Our children have always loved to hear stories over and over again!

If you don't wish to use it as part of a day-to-day curriculum, just read your child the stories, answer the questions, and implement the practical projects as desired. *Character Concepts Curriculum* is available for preschool through high school at www. thelearningparent.com.

REMEMBER: coloring pages are available online for
use with this book. Just go to our website:
www.thelearning parent.com
add *Character Trails Coloring Pages* to your cart,
proceed to checkout and use code COLOR,
and they will be free!

CONTENTS

Attentiveness   **9**

Samuel   *10*

Lydia Darragh   *12*

Afternoon at the Farm   *15*

Availability   **23**

Isaiah   *24*

Gunnar Kaasen & Balto   *26*

"Lauren, Availability!"   *30*

Boldness   **37**

Shadrach, Meshach & Abednego   *38*

Ethan Allen   *41*

Hide-and-Seek   *43*

Compassion   **51**

David and Mephibosheth   *52*

Florence Nightingale   *54*

Spending Time   *57*

Courage   **63**

Daniel   *64*

Jacob DeShazer   *66*

Standing Alone for Righteousness   *69*

Decisiveness   **75**

King Solomon   *76*

General Robert E. Lee   *78*

Popcorn   *81*

Endurance 87

Peter & John before the Sanhedrin 88
Daniel Boone 90
A Splash in a Pond 93

Flexibility 101

Paul Changes Plans 102
General Douglas MacArthur 104
Cassidy Makes a Choice 107

Generosity 115

The Good Samaritan 116
Andrew Carnegie 118
Seven Dollars to Spend 121

Joyfulness 129

Paul and Silas in Prison 130
Fanny Crosby 132
God's Plan 135

Orderliness 143

King Solomon Builds the Temple 144
James Madison 146
In an Orderly Way 148

Thoroughness 155

King Josiah Destroys the Idols 156
Dr. William Gorgas 158
Good Work! 160

Samuel Talks to God
1 Samuel 3

ATTENTIVENESS

LISTENING WITH THE EARS,
EYES, AND HEART

"The ear that heareth the reproof of life abideth among the wise."

—Proverbs 15:31

"My son, attend to my words; incline thine ear unto my sayings. Let them not depart from thine eyes; keep them in the midst of thine heart."

—Proverbs 4:20-21

ATTENTIVENESS

IN THE BIBLE

Samuel Talks with God

A long time ago, there lived an Israelite boy named Samuel, who served the Lord by helping Eli, the high priest. In those days it was rare to receive a special message from the Lord.

One night, when Eli had gone to bed and Samuel was sleeping in the temple beside the Ark of God, Samuel heard a voice call, "Samuel!"

Even though Samuel had been sleeping, he said, "Yes? What is it?" and got up.

He ran to Eli, because he thought it was Eli who had called him.

"Here I am," Samuel said. "Did you call me?"

"No, I didn't call you," said Eli. "Go back to bed." So Samuel went back to bed.

Again a voice called, "Samuel!" and again, Samuel went immediately to ask Eli whether he had called.

But Eli had not called, and again he sent Samuel back to bed.

You see, Samuel didn't know it was the Lord's voice calling him, because he had never had a message from the Lord before.

The voice called a third time, and Samuel ran a third time to ask Eli whether he had called. This time, Eli realized that Samuel was being called by the voice of the Lord God Himself.

So Eli told Samuel to go back to bed, and this time, if anyone called him to say, "Speak, Lord, your servant is listening."

Samuel obeyed Eli, and when the Lord called a fourth time, he was ready to answer:

"Speak, your servant is listening."

Then the Lord gave Samuel a terrible message about Eli and his family, because Eli had failed to discipline his sons, and now they were blaspheming the holy name of God.

Samuel was afraid to give this message to Eli, but the next day, when Eli insisted that he tell him what the Lord had said, Samuel told him.

"It is the Lord's will," said Eli. "Let Him do what he thinks best."

From that day forth, Samuel remained attentive to the voice of the Lord, and everything that Samuel said was true, because it came from God. Everyone in Israel knew that Samuel listened to the Lord.

ATTENTIVENESS

IN HISTORY

Lydia Darragh

In the year 1777, a little old Quaker woman did a very brave thing: at the risk of her own life, she brought secret information to the American army. Her name was Lydia Darragh.

It happened that during the month of December, the British army demanded to stay in the house of Mr. Darragh. The Darragh family, however, had nowhere else to go themselves, so Lydia went to ask if they would have mercy on them. The general of the British army agreed that the family could stay in the house; and the army would only use one room for meetings.

One night, the general told Lydia to get her family in bed by eight o'clock because the army was going to have a meeting in her house that night. They would wake her up when they were done so she could let them out of the house.

All of the family went to sleep, except for attentive Lydia, who snuck into a closet nearby the room in which the meeting was being held. She was able to hear the final review of the meeting, and learned that British army intended a certain attack on the American camp in just a few days. Her own son, Charles, was at that American camp. She feared for the American army, and determined to do something.

She went back to bed, and didn't answer the British soldiers' knocks until the third or fourth time so that they would believe she had been asleep. She let them out of the house, and waited to act until daytime.

On December 4, 1777, Lydia Darragh took the secret information she had learned, and using a pass she had gotten, bravely crossed the British lines. She met with Colonel Craig on her way to the American camp, and she told him what she had learned. It is assumed that she also gave information to General

Boudinot in a needle-book, delivered to him by another old woman.

At any rate, the information was given to General George Washington, and he was able to act in time to prepare his army against the attack of the British. Who knows what may have happened, had Lydia Darragh not been so brave and attentive?

ATTENTIVENESS

IN EVERYDAY LIFE

Afternoon at the Farm

"**C**ome people of the risen King, who delight to bring Him praise!" Lauren sang loudly. Anne covered her ears. "Lauren," she asked meekly, "do you ever stop singing?" "Not much!" Lauren replied. "Come all and tune your hearts to sing to the Morning Star of grace!"

Anne grimaced. Aunt Grace laughed from the front seat of her car. "Hey Laur," she said, with the intent of distracting. "Which horse are you going to ride today?"

"I think I'm going to ride Flip." Lauren replied.

"What about you, Anne?"

"I want to ride Dixie." Anne said. "She's my favorite. Although, if Grandad had a pinto, I would ride that. Pintos are my favorite kind of horses."

Grace grinned again. Anne had wanted Grandad to purchase a pinto for a long time now. The girls chattered happily for the rest of the ride.

Arriving at the farm, they piled out of the car and ran to the hay loft to play while Grace caught and saddled the horses. "I'm going to swing on the rope swing!" Anne called. "Ooh, me too! Wait for me!" Lauren cried.

After awhile they heard Grace calling their names. They peeked out the window in the hay loft. "I'm ready!" Grace called. With squeals of delight, the girls ran down the stairs and over to the barn where the horses were kept.

"Before we ride," Grace told them, "there are a few things I need to tell you, and I need you to listen carefully. The horses get spooked easily by loud noises, so we must be very careful to be quiet and gentle around them. We can't yell or sing loudly or anything like that or they may take off running. And we would then take a tumble!" Anne and Lauren giggled.

"But seriously, girls," Grace continued, "I need you to remember what I've told you. Let's see how attentively you were listening. What did I tell you we cannot do around the horses?"

"Yell!" Lauren replied.

"Or sing loudly, or anything like that," Anne added, glancing at Lauren. "Very good," Grace said. "Now let's ride!" She helped them mount their horses, then took the reins for each to lead them along. Lauren giggled excitedly. "I love riding horses!" she said. "Don't sing about it," Anne cautioned.

Lauren frowned. "I know, Anne. I heard what Aunt Grace said. I listened attentively too!" The horses took off across the field as Grace led them, and Anne and Lauren grinned from ear to ear. There was just something about riding across the fields

or through the woods that the girls loved. They felt as if they were sitting up on top of the world!

The three spent most of the afternoon at the farm. Sometimes Grace would hop up on one of their horses with them and they would ride double for awhile, while she held the other horse's reins and led them along side by side. Sometimes she walked ahead. The girls laughed and talked and enjoyed themselves immensely.

Finally it was time to go, and the cousins watched as Grace unsaddled the horses, brushed them, and sent them out into the pasture. On the way home, Grace praised the girls for being careful and quiet around the horses. "You both listened attentively and obeyed very well," Grace said. "And now we are going back to my house and you both get to play until your moms pick you up."

"Hooray!" the girls shouted.

ATTENTIVENESS

IN YOUR LIFE

Questions

1. You normally sit with Mom and Dad in church. How might you strive to be attentive during the sermon?

2. How can you help lead your younger brothers/sisters to show attentiveness during family devotions?

3. Mom is going grocery shopping and giving you last minute instructions of what she wants you to get accomplished while she is gone. You are reading a book while she is giving you directions. What should you do to be more attentive?

Practical Projects

1. Buy your child a special notebook for taking notes in church.

2. Have your child ask your pastor what he will be preaching about the following week. Read this passage to your child for family devotions on Saturday night. (My daughter-in-law printed a denarius from a website for Luke to hold on Sunday while the pastor was preaching on a passage about a denarius)

3. Have a family Bible quiz night (we used to do this every Friday night). Supply treats for questions answered correctly. Use Bible

questions from passages you read during family devotions or Bible stories this week. It causes the kids to really become attentive and pay close attention as you read. They want to be able to answer the questions correctly. (We offer a sample Family Bible Quiz on our website with answers provided—www.thelearningparent.com.)

Isaiah: "Here Am I, Send Me!"
Isaiah 6

AVAILABILITY

BEING WILLING TO ATTEND TO A NEED
WHEN I AM CALLED TO HELP

"Also I heard the voice of the Lord, saying, 'Whom shall I send, and who will go for us?' Then said I, 'Here am I; send me.' "

–Isaiah 6:8

23

AVAILABILITY

IN THE BIBLE

Here Am I, Send Me!

saiah was a prophet to the nation of Judah, and to the city of Jerusalem. He had many visions and spoke many prophecies to the hard-hearted people, and in the end he was executed by those who would not listen to God. It would seem he had a difficult and perhaps even a fruitless life, but he did not. He lived it in obedience to God, following the calling that God had for him.

It all started in the year that King Uzziah died. Isaiah had a vision of the Lord sitting on a throne, and the Lord's robe was filling the Temple. There were seraphim praising the Lord's name.

At first, Isaiah thought that he would die, because he was a filthy sinner, and the Lord God was far too holy for him to look upon and live. However, God sent one of the seraphim to tell Isaiah that his sins were forgiven.

Then the Lord asked, "Whom shall I send to be

a messenger to my people in Judah? Who will go for us?"

Isaiah did not think, "Well, I can't, because I already have plans for my life," or, "I can't, because it's going to be a very difficult job."

No, instead he made himself available for the Lord to use, for whatever the Lord wanted to. Isaiah said, "Here I am. Send me."

So the Lord told Isaiah that Isaiah would be a prophet. He told Isaiah that the people would not listen to him, but that he must preach to them the words of God anyway. Isaiah would have to tell the people of Judah about the judgment that was coming on them for their rebellion. God was sending this judgment to cleanse their nation because He loved them.

It is never fun to be the bearer of bad news, but Isaiah was willing to be God's prophet because he feared the Lord. He knew that he was only the clay and the Lord was the potter; it was his duty to be available for whatever the Lord needed.

AVAILABILITY

IN HISTORY

Gunnar Kaasen and the Story of Balto

Gunnar Kaasen was available when the lives of hundreds of people hung in the balance. The things he and his sled dogs endured in order to help the dying people of Nome, Alaska, were truly grueling.

The Native Americans that lived in the small settlement of Nome had become very sick. They were not used to the sicknesses that the white men had—in this case, diphtheria—and it was killing them. They needed medicine badly.

The problem was that no airplanes could get to them, because in those days the only airplanes in their area had open cockpits. No one would be able to fly in bitterly cold Alaska with an open cockpit. The train could only get to a town that was days away from Nome. The only ones who could bring the medicine to the sick people were the "mush-

26

ers," men who rode on sleds through the snow pulled by a team of dogs.

Several teams of man and dogs braved the fierce cold to bring the medicine to Nome. One team would bring the medicine to another team, and so on, like a relay race. It was a race to save people's lives.

The second-to-last team was led by a man named Gunnar Kaasen. His lead dog, Balto, was not the best leader, but Balto was what Gunnar had. As they were riding across the snow, they were met by a terrible blizzard.

There was nothing a man could do to find his way through the fury of wind and snow—it was up to Balto now. At one point, the team would have met its death in the Topkok River had not Balto saved them all.

When the team had miraculously reached

Gunnar Kaasen and Balto

the last stop, Gunnar found that the last man was asleep! Gunnar and his dogs must have wanted rest more than ever before in all their lives, and certainly they deserved it.

But who, then, would take the medicine to Nome? Gunnar decided to finish the race himself, and he and his dogs set out to Nome. They didn't have time to waste if they were going to help the dying people.

Balto and the sled team

On the way, they were met by a powerful wind that took the whole sled, including the dogs, into the air. When they landed with a jolt, the precious medicine was lost in the snow! Gunnar frantically searched in the snow, and he was able to find the medicine.

They reached Nome in record time, and delivered the medicine safely to the doctor who lived there. No more of the Native Americans died after that. The diphtheria was stopped.

Of course, you and I know that it was God Almighty who saved the people of Nome. Only He could have made it possible for the teams to break record time in their race. Only He could have made it possible for Balto to lead the sled through the storm, and for Gunnar to find the lost medicine in the snow. God was able to use Balto and Gunnar because Gunnar Kaasen and his team were available when help was needed.

Nome, Alaska

AVAILABILITY

IN EVERYDAY LIFE

"Lauren, Availability!"

Lauren **was a very busy little girl**. In fact, there were so many things she wanted to do, she didn't know how she would ever get them all done in a day. Playing with her dollhouse, swinging on her swing outside, visiting Nana's house to see all her aunts, uncles, cousins, and the pets… the options were endless!

She was also a very vocal little girl, and most days would sing as she played, did her chores, or even just walked around the house. Even though she knew a lot of songs that she had learned at church or that her mom had taught her, she sometimes ran out, and had to make up her own.

On one such day, she was crawling under her bed to see what treasures she could find hidden under there and making up words to songs as she sang…very loudly.

"Lauren!" called her mom. Lauren jumped, hitting her head on the bed. "Ouch!" she whispered,

as she scooted back out and replied, "Yes, mommy?"

"It's time to do your school work," her mom said. "Come on into the kitchen please." Lauren was a little disappointed, because she was just sure that she had been about to find the best treasure ever, but she got up anyway, and went into the kitchen.

Her school work was fun after all. She was learning how to write her letters, and had already mastered spelling her name. She also knew how to do a lot of other things. She loved history, and could quote from memory stories of many significant men and women throughout history. Her favorite time, though, was when her mom picked

up the Bible and began to read. There were so many neat stories in the Bible that she loved to listen to. Lauren listened intently this morning, as her mom read to her from Isaiah 6. She didn't understand all of it, but one thing she noticed was in verse 8, when the Lord was looking for someone to go give the people a message for Him. Isaiah, though he must have been very busy with all his work as a prophet, stepped right up and said, "Here am I! Send me."

"Mommy?" asked Lauren. "That was pretty good that he said 'send me' wasn't it? I mean, he must have been really busy, but he was willing to go right then anyway!"

"That's right Lauren," Her mom said. "Isaiah knew that God's work was most important. He had also learned a very important quality called 'Availability'." She went on to explain that availability meant being willing to attend to a need when you are called to help someone. Lauren thought about that for awhile.

That afternoon, she and her mom drove over to her cousin Cassidy's house to pick up some dishes her mom had left there. "Lauren," her mom began, "will you help Cass and Adam take care of baby James for a minute please? I have something I need to talk to your Aunt Kari about."

"Oh, but Mommy, Cass and I were going to go back and jump on the trampoline! We can't do that if we're watching James. Could you watch him for a little while, and then we'll watch him?"

Her mom's face grew serious. "Lauren, first of all, you need to obey Mommy cheerfully and immediately when she asks you to do something. And secondly, do you remember what we were talking about with Isaiah this morning?"

Lauren thought for a minute. "Oh yeah—availability!" she remembered. "I'm sorry, Mommy.

Sure, I'll watch James. Here am I, send me!" she giggled, and took James's hand to lead him off to play. Her mom smiled and went back to talking to Aunt Kari.

The four cousins enjoyed their playtime, and soon it was time for Lauren to go. As they were in the car, Lauren said, "Hey, Mommy? You remember when I wasn't being available when you needed me? I'm sorry. And next time, all you have to say is, 'Lauren, availability!' and I'll remember to do what's right!" Her mom smiled. "Thank you Lauren," she said. "I may just try that."

AVAILABILITY

IN YOUR LIFE

Questions

1. Mom is fixing supper and your baby sister is very fussy. How could you demonstrate availability in this situation?
2. You were planning to make a cardboard airplane this afternoon from your new kit but Dad needs someone to help him train the dog. How could you practice availability?
3. The home school group is looking for two more volunteers to fill Operation Christmas Child boxes to send overseas to needy children. How might you practice availability in this situation?

Practical Projects

1. Help your child to watch for a specific way to practice availability this week.
2. Lead your child in being available to fulfill a need of an elderly person at church, helping them plan and prepare. Teach them how to listen for hints of things that the person likes or needs for future ministry to them.
3. Praise your child when you see him/her purposefully making themselves available to meet someone else's need.
4. Make a list of things your child could do to demonstrate availability within your family, your neighborhood, your church, your community.

Shadrach, Meshach, and Abednego
Daniel 3

BOLDNESS

**FACING CONFRONTATIONS
WITH THE ASSURANCE THAT
GOD WILL BLESS THE OUTCOME
IF I'M STANDING FOR THE TRUTH**

*"The wicked flee when no man pursueth: but the
righteous are bold as a lion."*

—Proverbs 28:1

BOLDNESS

IN THE BIBLE

Shadrach, Meshach, and Abednego

Nebuchadnezzar was king over all of Babylon. The Babylonians had conquered Israel, and had taken many captives back to Babylon with them. Among these captives were Daniel and three other young men: Hananiah, Mishael, and Azariah, whose names were changed to Shadrach, Meshach, and Abednego.

All four of them were soon given high positions in the Babylonian kingdom, because they were so trustworthy and because their God, the one true God, was watching over them.

It happened that the king had a gigantic golden statue of himself made, and he set it up in a place called Dura. He commanded that all of his officials throughout the kingdom should come and worship it. Shadrach, Meshach, and Abednego were forced to attend the ceremony as well, and it was decreed that anyone who didn't bow to the statue would be thrown into a fiery furnace.

The three young Jews, however, knew that they could not bow down and worship a mere statue for they believed in the God of their fathers, the only true and living God. He alone is worthy of worship. So when the instruments played, and all the other officials around them were bowing down, these three men did not, but boldly stood their ground.

The king was extremely angry. He didn't immediately order them thrown into the furnace, because he liked them so much. Instead, he had them brought before him, and he offered them one more chance to obey his decree.

But Shadrach, Meshach, and Abednego gave him fair warning that they would never bow down to the statue, nor worship any of the Babylonian gods. Moreover, they told him that their God was powerful enough to rescue them from the fiery furnace, if it were His will.

King Nebuchadnezzar's face was twisted with anger as he commanded that the furnace be made seven times hotter, and that the strongest men of his army throw these three bold Jews into the flames. It was done, but the hot fire killed the strong soldiers even as they threw Shadrach, Meshach, and Abednego into it. Surely, those three could not survive.

Much to the king's amazement, however, they were not dead! They were walking about, and there was a fourth person walking with them. Nebuchadnezzar was so astonished and amazed that he ordered the young men to come out of the fire, calling them "servants of the Most High God."

Shadrach, Meshach, and Abednego came out. Everyone saw that their clothes were not burnt, their hair not singed—they didn't even smell like smoke!

And Nebuchadnezzar, that heathen king, praised their God, the one true God. He was able to see that the God of Israel was alive and real and powerful, because of the boldness of Shadrach, Meshach, and Abednego, and God's miracle on their behalf.

BOLDNESS

IN HISTORY

Ethan Allen

Ethan Allen and the Green Mountain Boys were legendary in New England.

They had been fighting for the rights of land, which is now the state of Vermont, for some time. They were a well-organized group of patriots that wanted nothing to do with British rule.

So during the Revolutionary War, Ethan Allen was asked to bring his Green Mountain Boys to lead an attack on Fort Ticonderoga, New York. On May 10, 1775, the men, along with some of the Connecticut militia, would surprise the fort before dawn.

Allen and his men stealthily crossed a lake by boat during the night; and

statue of Ethan Allen

41

then, as the sun began to light up the eastern sky, the bold attack was launched.

Ethan Allen himself did not waste his time fighting, but went as soon as he could to the place where the commander of the fort was sleeping. He was going to make the commander surrender. The commander's right-hand man met Ethan first, however, and demanded Ethan tell in whose name he was doing this.

"In the name of the Great Jehovah and the Continental Congress!" cried Ethan Allen.

The commander of the fort then came out of his room, and surrendered his sword and the fort to Ethan Allen. Because of Ethan's boldness, the British hardly knew what had hit them, and not a single shot was fired.

BOLDNESS

IN EVERYDAY LIFE

Hide and Seek

Luke was outside playing with Melody and his Aunt Kelley one day in Nana's back yard. The cousins loved to play hide and seek in the yard because there were a lot of good hiding spots.

"Your turn to be 'it,' Kell!" Luke said. "Mommy said I have 20 minutes to play before I have to go to watch Michael."

"OK, go hide!" Kelley replied, as she covered her face with her hands and began counting. "1, 2, 3…" Melo-

dy ran to hide behind the wood pile. That was a good place because you could look out between the logs, but whoever was searching couldn't see you!

43

Luke looked around for a hiding place. Ah! He spotted the pine trees in the neighboring yard. "Those will be the perfect place to hide! She will never find me there!" Luke thought, as he scurried into the trees just as he heard Kelley calling, "Ready or not, here I come!" He ducked underneath some of the bigger ones, crouched down, and waited.

Kelley began searching the yard. "I'm coming to get you!" she called. "You'd better be in some good hiding places!"

Melody giggled, then clapped her hand over her mouth. "I heard that!" Kell called. She headed towards the wood pile as Melody held her breath. Kell looked behind the cedar tree, then behind the shed. No sign of Mel. All of a sudden, she poked her head behind the wood pile. "Found you!" she called.

Melody laughed as Kelley caught her up and tickled her. "Now you have to go find Luke!" she said. "Ah, right you are!" Kell respond- ed, and re- sumed her search. A few min- utes later, she looked around, puzzled. I can't seem

to find him, Mel. Do you know where he is?"

"I think I saw something moving in the neigh- bors' trees," Mel whispered.

"Hmm. It may have been a cat or something, but we'll check."

They moved towards the trees, just as Luke jumped out and yelled. "Oh! You scared me!" Kel- ley said. "Me too!" added Melody. "I jumped!"

Luke laughed. "Wasn't that a good hiding place?" "It was," Kelley began, "but Luke, look at that." She pointed into the trees, and Luke noticed that there were a couple of small pine trees lying flat on the ground. "Oops," he said. "I didn't know I did that. But it doesn't really matter, right? They don't really care about the little trees when they have all of these big ones, do they?"

Kelley looked disappointed. "These are the baby trees, Luke." She explained. "They were just planted this year. You see, some of the older ones had died so they planted new ones to take their places. And now it appears that they will have a few less new ones too." Luke looked at it and thought a minute. "I really think we need to go talk to the neighbors." Kelley said. "You can explain to them what happened and apologize. I'm sure they will appreciate your honesty, and if there is something they can do to make these trees grow again, we need to tell them now."

Luke struggled within himself. "I don't want to do that!" he thought. "Mr. Kennedy seems kind of scary, and besides, I really don't want to have to tell them I trampled their trees! I'm scared!"

"I don't want to," he told Kelley. "I know," Kell responded in an understanding tone. "It can be hard to make things right after we have done wrong or hurt someone else's property. It is rarely something we want to do. But don't you want to do what is right?"

"Well . . . I do, but I'm scared," Luke admitted. "What if they get mad at me?"

"Come here, Luke," Kelley said, putting her arm around him. Let me tell you a Bible verse I learned one time. It is Proverbs 28:1. 'The wicked flee when no one pursues, but the righteous are bold as a lion.' You see, it is not going to be easy, but we must choose to do what is right; and we can be bold in it, for we both know that this is what God would want you to do. His Word tells us that He will bless us when we obey Him, so let's trust in Him and choose to do what is right."

Luke thought for a minute. "Okay," he agreed. "You're right, Kell. I know this is what God wants me to do, so I will try to be bold and trust him. Let's go."

The three trooped up to the neighbor's house and rang the doorbell. Mr. Kennedy opened the door. Luke gulped. He was tempted to run away, but he remembered, that is what wicked people do. He wanted to be a bold and righteous boy, so he stayed. He swallowed, and then told Mr. Kennedy everything.

Mr. Kennedy smiled. "Luke," he said, "I just want you to know, I really appreciate your honesty. There are not many boys your age who would be bold enough to come and apologize for such a thing. I commend you for that, and seeing such honesty—even when I am sure it was difficult to be so—is worth a few trampled trees to me." Luke breathed a sigh of relief. "Thank you," he replied. "But actually, it was my Aunt Kelley who convinced me to do what was right. And a Bible verse she told me about."

Luke skipped along the path back to Nana's house to play with Michael. He felt light as a feather! All was well now, Mr. Kennedy was not angry, and Luke had done what was right.

BOLDNESS

IN YOUR LIFE

Questions

1. Some big boys are teasing your little brother. How can you show boldness by standing up for righteousness?

2. Your neighbor is going off to war. He isn't a Christian. How can you demonstrate boldness in a loving way by sharing the gospel with him (or giving a gift of a Bible)?

3. The neighborhood kids are throwing stones at a kitty. How can you demonstrate boldness in protecting the innocent and influencing them to do right?

Practical Projects

1. Teach your child how to share the gospel and choose a neighbor or acquaintance to visit and share with.

2. Buy your child some tracts or let him/her write their own tract and choose opportune places to leave them.

3. Encourage your child to speak God's truth when friends or siblings are doing wrong, not condemning them, but not being embarrassed to identify with Christ.

David and Mephibosheth
2 Samuel 9 and 19

COMPASSION

BEING WILLING TO EXPEND EFFORT TO HELP ALLEVIATE THE SUFFERING OF THOSE IN NEED

"Withhold not good from them to whom it is due, when it is in the power of thine hand to do it."
—Proverbs 3:27

COMPASSION

IN THE BIBLE

David and Mephibosheth

As you may remember, King Saul had hated David for a long time, and tried many times to kill him. This was because Saul was jealous of David, because David had received the Lord's anointing to replace Saul as king.

Saul's son Jonathan was David's best friend. They promised they would always take care of each other and their families, no matter what. Saul and Jonathan were both killed in battle, and David became king just as the Lord had planned. When he was settled he asked, "Is there still anyone who is left of the house of Saul, that I may show him kindness for Jonathan's sake?" His servants brought Jonathan's son Mephibosheth to David. Mephibosheth had been crippled in an accident when he was a child. David showed compassion and gave him the land that had belonged to Saul, and had him eat at the king's table every day. However, Mephibosheth's servant Ziba was jealous because he wanted Saul's land, and he plotted to cause trouble between Mephibosheth and David.

Many years later, David's son Absalom plotted to harm David and steal the kingdom. David was forced to leave Jerusalem for a time. Soon after David returned, Mephibosheth came to meet him. Mephibosheth told David that his servant Ziba had deceived him in order to get Saul's land and had prevented him from going with David into exile. It must have been frightening for Mephibosheth to visit the king, because David was angry that Mephibosheth had abandoned him. However, David listened and believed him.

Needless to say, Mephibosheth was very grateful. David decided to divide the land equally between Mephibosheth and Ziba. But by this time, Mephibosheth no longer cared; he was so overcome by David's great compassion.

"Just give all the land to Ziba," he said. "I am only glad to have you safely back again, my king!"

COMPASSION

IN HISTORY

Florence Nightingale

Florence Nightingale could have had a very easy life, if she had only wished it. She was born into a family that had money, respect, and important friends. However, Florence was called by God for another purpose. When she was still a very young woman, she knew that He had called her to be a nurse.

Nurses back then were not like the ones you are used to. Nursing was not a career in those days; it was a lowly job. Florence taught herself as much as she could about nursing. Her family and friends were not happy about this decision of hers, but she did it anyway, because she knew it was what God wanted her to do. She had felt compassion for the sick and needy ever since she was a small child.

Britain was in the middle of a war in a country then called Crimea. The British soldiers in the hospital there were dying at tremendous rates,because the hospitals were so dirty and under-staffed. The soldiers had no blankets or good food. Many of them were left in their stiff, dirty uniforms because there was no one to take care of them.

In 1854, Florence went to Crimea, along with other nurses, to help the dying soldiers. She was shocked and very sad at the poor conditions that the soldiers had to endure. She pleaded with the British government for help, but they would not listen to her advice.

The soldiers were encouraged by the sight of her walking the hallways, looking for someone to help. She would even stay up late into the night, walking the hallways with a lamp in her hand. The soldiers began to call her the "Lady with the Lamp."

The "Lady with the Lamp" became famous back in Britain for her compassion and her good work in

Florence Nightingale

Crimea. This fame allowed her to publish pamphlets about the awful conditions of the hospitals in Crimea. Her fame won her lots of support, and the government was obliged to send her the aid she needed.

She made the hospitals cleaner for the soldiers, and soon enough there were fewer and fewer men dying, and more and more getting better.

When Florence returned to England she was very popular. She wrote books about how important it was for hospitals to be clean. There was even a school founded in her name to teach nursing. To this day, Florence Nightingale is known for her bravery and her great compassion.

Florence Nightingale,
The "Lady with the Lamp"

COMPASSION

IN EVERYDAY LIFE

Spending Time

Anne was five years old. She lived with her mom and dad, her little brother Patrick, and her new baby sister, Ella. Although, Anne never just called her Ella. To her, the baby was always Ella Rose. Anne was proud that she had helped pick out the name for her baby sister, you see, and she thought that it would be a shame to not call her by both of her names, because they were so pretty.

Anne loved to hold her baby sister, and spent lots of time helping her mom take care of the baby. Taking care of a baby can be hard work, but there is a lot that a big girl like Anne can do!

Anne also spent a lot of time playing with Patrick, while her mom was tending to Ella Rose. Patrick didn't quite understand why this new baby was taking so much of his mom's attention all of a sudden, so Anne tried to explain to him that Mom had to spend just as much time taking care of him when he was a baby too.

One day poor Patrick was very sick. He had a fever and a runny nose, and he just didn't feel good at all. Anne got up that morning eagerly looking forward to holding baby Ella for a long time that day. But then she saw Patrick. He looked so sad, and though Mom was trying to be with him as much as she could, she also had to take care of the baby.

Anne thought for a few minutes, then she went to her room. She found a little bag and filled it with stickers and small toys. Then she brought it to Patrick. "Here you go, Buddy!" she said. "I brought you a present to help you feel better!"

Now even when little boys don't feel well, they still like presents, and Patrick was no exception. He opened the bag and when he saw what was inside, he smiled. Anne smiled back. Then she said, Now,

 would you like me to read some stories to you?" "Da!" That was how Patrick said 'yes.'

Anne got out some of their favorite story books and showed her little brother the pictures as she read along. In some of the books, the words were too hard to read, so she just made up a story to go along with the pictures. Before too long it was lunch time, and Anne brought Buddy some food and a drink. Then she lay down on the couch with him and sang to him until he fell asleep. Later in the afternoon, after he woke up, Anne brought in some paper and crayons and they colored pictures and decorated them with the stickers Anne had brought that morning.

When it was time for Anne to go to bed that night, her mom came in to tuck her in. "Where's Ella Rose?" Anne asked.

"Daddy is taking care of her," her mom replied. "Anne," she continued, "I'm really proud of you for the compassion you showed to Patrick today. You could have been playing with your toys or holding the baby, but instead you chose to give your time to take care of your brother and help him feel better. The Bible talks a lot about being kind to one another, and loving one another not just in words, but in deeds—what we do—and you certainly did that today. Thank you for helping me and showing compassion to your brother."

Anne smiled. "You're welcome, Mom," she said. "I do love Buddy, and I'm glad I could help him and I'm going to pray tonight that God will help him get better." They bowed their heads, as Anne prayed for her little brother; then her mom prayed, and thanked God for the spirit of compassion He had given to her little girl.

COMPASSION

IN YOUR LIFE

Questions

1. Your friend was trying to help you get the cap off your water bottle. He twisted a little too hard and water went flying all over the kitchen. How can you demonstrate compassion?

2. Your little sister has to go to the doctor for her shots. She is scared and crying. What might you do to show her compassion?

3. Your friend's grandfather just went to heaven. What some ways you could show compassion to him?

Practical Projects

1. Help your child to make a card for someone who is sick.

2. Find a mom who just had a baby. Invite her other children over for the day and plan a special day for them.

3. Look for opportunities to show compassion:
   • brother skinned his knee
   • friend whose mom miscarried
   • neighbor whose spouse just died

Daniel in the Lion's Den, Courageously Praying
Because He Knew it was Right
Daniel 6

COURAGE

STANDING ALONE FOR RIGHTEOUSNESS

"Have not I commanded thee? Be strong and of a good courage; be not afraid, neither be thou dismayed: for the LORD thy God is with thee whithersoever thou goest."

—Joshua 1:9

COURAGE

IN THE BIBLE

Daniel in the Lions' Den

Daniel was an administrator for Darius, who was king over the united empire of Media and Persia. King Darius was so impressed by Daniel that he planned to give Daniel authority over all the empire.

This made some of the king's other administrators jealous, and so they began to look for ways to get Daniel into trouble. However, they couldn't find anything that Daniel did wrong, because he was a godly man, faithful, responsible, and trustworthy. So the jealous administrators came up with a deceptive scheme to get Daniel into trouble for doing something *right*.

They got King Darius to make a law that for 30 days the people of the empire could only pray to the king. If they prayed to anyone else, they would be thrown into a den of lions.

Daniel had always prayed three times every day to the Lord God. He believed that God was worthy of his worship, and he knew that God would be displeased if he worshipped anyone else. So Daniel prayed three times to God the very day that the law was signed, despite the terrible risk. It must have taken a great deal of courage for him to do that.

Those who were jealous of Daniel were watching him closely, because they knew he would disobey this law. When they saw him praying, they ran to King Darius to tattle on Daniel.

Although King Darius liked Daniel very much, he could not change the law now, and so he was forced by his own words to throw Daniel into the lions' den. He earnestly wished that God would rescue Daniel because of Daniel's faithfulness.

Daniel was in the lions' den overnight, but the lions did not hurt him, because God kept their ferocious mouths tightly shut. As soon as it was morning, King Darius ran to the den to see whether Daniel was alive. How glad he was that Daniel had not received so much as a scratch!

Then the king had the jealous administrators and their families thrown into the lions' den themselves—and God did not protect them from their deserved fate.

Daniel, on the other hand, prospered. King Darius saw that Daniel's God was the living God with an everlasting reign, because of Daniel's faithfulness and courage.

COURAGE

IN HISTORY

Jacob DeShazer

On December 7, 1941, something happened that shook America like nothing had for many years. It was World War II, but the Americans didn't expect that the Japanese would bomb Pearl Harbor, a U.S. naval base in Hawaii.

The attack was shocking, devastating, and enraging. Among those who vowed to get revenge on the Japanese for this act was a man named Jacob DeShazer.

"The Japs are going to have to pay for this!" he exclaimed when he heard the news of the surprise attack on Pearl Harbor.

And, indeed, he went on to join a military force that was formed specifically for bombarding the Japanese. He was assigned to fly over Japan, dropping bombs in the wake of his airplane. But when the mission was complete, he found that his airplane was running out of fuel. The plane went down in China, and he and his men were forced to parachute out of it to save themselves. When they landed, they were captured by none other than Japanese soldiers.

The men were kept in P.O.W. camps for three-and-a-half years, beaten, starved, and some even killed outright. DeShazer was the only survivor when the war finally ended and he was rescued by U.S. troops.

While he was in prison, DeShazer got hold of a Bible. He became a firm Christian, and upon his return to the United States, he began studying to be a missionary. He was going to go back to preach the Gospel in Japan. God had done a wonderful work in his heart.

Just a few years after the World War, Jacob DeShazer and his wife moved to Japan, where he began to faithfully preach the Gospel to the very nation that had hurt his own. It must have taken immense courage to make a stand for God in this place that hated the Americans, in this place where

Jacob DeShazer

Mitsuo Fuchida

he had been beaten and starved only a short time before.

Eventually, De-Shazer came to meet Captain Mitsuo Fuchida, the very same man who had led the attack on Pearl Harbor in 1941. These two former enemies actually became friends! Moreover, the Japanese captain also came to a saving knowledge of the Lord when he read a Gospel tract about Jacob DeShazer's own conversion. Captain Fuchida also became a missionary to his people, and he and DeShazer preached the Gospel in Japan together.

Only God could have turned such hatred into such love, and only God could have given Jacob the courage he needed to be a friend to his enemies.

Mitsuo Fuchida and Jacob DeShazer

COURAGE

IN EVERYDAY LIFE

Standing Alone for Righteousness

On Friday nights, all the Boyer cousins and their families gathered at Nana and Granddad's house for dinner. Everyone loved these opportunities to spend time together as a family, laughing, talking, and eating. The cousins loved to play together, whether outside or in the basement playing dress-up, race cars, or whatever was the game of choice for that evening.

One particular Friday night, several

of the cousins were out playing in the yard when one of them suggested they climb up into the tree house and play war.

"Yeah!" cried Luke. "We can be the Americans and the British can be attacking! We can use sticks to be the guns and cannons. Come on, guys!" Everyone began to run for the tree house. Everyone, that is, except Adam.

Inside his heart, Adam was struggling. He wanted to play as much as any of the others, and he loved the tree house. It had a deck on top of the house, and that's where some of his cousins were headed. Yes, Adam very much wanted to join them. But Adam also

knew that one of the rules of Nana and Granddad's house was that no children were allowed in the tree house without an adult.

"But . . . it wasn't my idea," he reasoned with himself. "And everyone else is doing it. If it was that bad, they wouldn't all do it, right? I mean, does it really matter anyway?"

He started toward the tree house, drawn by the laughter of his cousins. But something inside him made him stop. He knew the right thing to do, but to do it would mean having to stand alone against all of his cousins in order to obey. He tried to tell himself that maybe they had all forgotten the rule. He tried hard to forget it himself, but to no avail.

Finally, Adam knew what he must do. He walked over to the tree house. "Hey guys," he began. "You may have forgotten, but Nana and Granddad said we aren't allowed to be in the tree house without an adult. I'd like to play with you all, but I can't disobey just so I can have fun. And really, I don't want any of you to get in trouble either, so . . . will you all come down and obey with me?"

He looked from cousin to cousin. They seemed to

be thinking. "OK," said Cassidy, and began scurrying down the ladder.

"I didn't forget," Cassidy admitted, "but I didn't want to be the only one that wouldn't climb up. I'm sorry. My disobedience must have made it even harder for you to obey, Adam."

Soon all the cousins had climbed down from the tree house. "Adam," Cassidy said, "Thanks for being courageous and standing up for what was right. The rest of us should have done the same thing. "

"That's right," added Luke. "We shouldn't have climbed up there at all."

"Now can we get ready for our battle?" asked Melody. As they all ran off to build earthworks in the sandbox, Adam breathed a sigh of relief. He knew God had helped him have courage to stand alone in doing what was right.

"Thank You, God!" he whispered, as he joined his cousins.

COURAGE

IN YOUR LIFE

Questions

1. The neighbor is yelling at you because he thinks your chickens ate up the seeds he just planted in his vegetable garden. How can you show courage?

2. Your friend is planning to do something wrong and tells you about it. How can you show courage?

3. Your chickens were in the neighbors' garden and uprooted some of their plants. How can you use courage to make it right?

Practical Projects

1. Assist your child in sharing the gospel with a neighbor or acquaintance. One idea could be to take them a tract and a nice dessert. Ask if there is any need in their life that your family can have the privilege of praying about.

2. Help your child work our correct responses for some instances you know they will encounter and need to use courage to face.

3. Have your child think of a person in Scripture who is an example of courage and read the account to your child. Think of more people in Scripture. Read in Joshua 1 what God told Joshua about courage.

Solomon Had Wisdom to Know
the Real Mom Would Want the Baby to Live
1 Kings 3

DECISIVENESS

THE ABILITY TO MAKE WISE DECISIONS BASED ON GOD'S STANDARDS

"But let him ask in faith, nothing wavering. For he that wavereth is like a wave of the sea driven with the wind and tossed."

—James 1:6

DECISIVENESS

IN THE BIBLE

King Solomon

Solomon was a very wise king. Because God had offered him anything he wanted and Solomon had chosen wisdom, God had blessed him with so much of it that Solomon was the wisest man who ever lived.

Countless times his wisdom helped him to make good decisions quickly. One such instance was the time that two women who were arguing with each other came to him for his help.

One of the women told him that they were arguing over which of them was the mother of the baby they had brought with them.

She said, "This other woman and I both had babies while living in the same house, very close to the same time. We were the only ones in the house. Then her baby died one night while we were sleeping; and she switched her baby with mine, who was alive. When I woke up, I found that my son was dead! But when I looked more closely, I realized that he was not my son."

The other woman interrupted her then, saying, "It was your son. This one is mine!"

"No," said the first woman, "this one is mine, and yours is dead."

They kept arguing back and forth like this, right in front of King Solomon.

Finally, Solomon put an end to their arguing with these decisive words, "All right, both of you think that this baby is yours, and that the dead one belongs to the other woman. Well, then, bring me a sword."

A servant brought a sword to the king.

"Now cut this child into two pieces, and we'll give a half to each mother."

The first woman, who was the real mother of the baby, screamed, "No! Please just give him to the other woman! Oh, don't kill him!" She would rather give him away than see him die, because she loved him very much.

The other woman, however, only said, "Fine, cut him in half! Then neither of us will get him," because she only wanted to win the argument; but she didn't love the child at all.

So Solomon, whose wisdom made plain to him which was the real mother, said, "Don't kill the baby. Give him to the first woman, because she wants him to live. She is his real mother!"

All of Israel heard this story about Solomon's decision. They all were amazed and praised God for giving their king such wisdom and justice.

DECISIVENESS

IN HISTORY

Robert E. Lee at Chancellorsville

It was the Civil War, 1863. The Union and the Confederacy were fighting a hard battle near a place called Chancellorsville, Virginia. General Robert E. Lee had a difficult decision to make.

Joseph Hooker was a general of the Union army, and Robert E. Lee was a general of the Confederate army. There were twice as many Union soldiers as there were Confederate soldiers. It seemed that all odds were against General Lee and his army.

Hooker's army crossed the Rapahannock and Rapidan Rivers to come against Lee's army on one side. Meanwhile, another Union general was trying to mess up the supplies being sent to General Lee's army from a distance. As if that wasn't enough, there was another Union army near Fredericksburg, not far away. They were going to attack General Lee and his men from front and back, so that there would be no escape.

Maybe most generals would have thought they needed every one of their men at Chancellorsville to keep from being destroyed. Maybe some of them would have surrendered, thinking there was no way out. But General Lee was sharp, and he made a seemingly strange decision while there was still time.

He decided to divide up his men. He sent a fifth of them to Fredericksburg, to distract one of the Union's armies, while the rest of his men would stay to fight it out with Hooker.

Hooker made the mistake of thinking the battle would easily be won. He had his army pull back and wait, allowing Lee to attack him. Because of

General Robert E. Lee

this, Lee's army was able to hold its own against Hooker's, despite all odds.

In the meantime, the Union won the battle in Fredericksburg against the rest of Lee's men. They began to make their way towards Chancellorsville.

However, the distraction Lee had planned had already worked. By the time this army reached Chancellorsville, Hooker's men were already losing badly. Lee's army turned around and sent the Union army from Fredericksburg flying! Hooker's army also turned tail and ran.

The Confederates won an astonishing victory that year, thanks to General Robert E. Lee's quick decisiveness.

Scene from the battle at Chancellorsville, Virginia, 1863

DECISIVENESS

IN EVERYDAY LIFE

Popcorn

Cassidy and Adam were jumping on the trampoline one day, talking and laughing and playing games as they jumped. "Adam, let's play popcorn!" Cassidy suggested.

"OK," agreed Adam. "You be the popcorn, and I'll try to pop you." Cassidy sat in the center of the trampoline with her legs crossed while Adam jumped in circles around her, trying to bounce her enough that her legs would come

uncrossed. "Wow, Sissy!" he finally said, as he dropped, breathless, onto the trampoline. "I don't think I can pop you! You're heavy!"

Cassidy jumped up laughing and said, "OK, I'll try to pop you then." "Just a minute!" Adam panted. "Let me catch my breath first."

She plopped down beside him on the trampo-line and they both laid back and looked up at the clouds. They tried to pick out different shapes and animals in the clouds.

"Look, that one could almost be a shoe!" Cass pointed out. "I like that one better," Adam said, gesturing in the other direction. "It reminds me of a cowboy hat."

"A cowboy hat?" Cass giggled. "I can't see that at all!" "That's 'cause you're a girl." Adam replied, getting up again.

As the two got up to continue their game, they noticed a car going down the road next to their yard. It was driving very slowly, and it came to a stop right across from where they sat on the tram-poline. "Who do you think that is?" Adam asked.

"I don't know." Cassidy replied. "I don't recognize them, do you?" Adam shook his head. As the two continued to watch the car, it started up again and continued down the road. "I guess they were just looking for somebody's house," Cassidy mused. "Come on, let's play!"

A few moments later, just as Cass succeeded in popping Adam, she glanced up to see the same car stopped next to them again. Cassidy began to get a bit nervous. "Adam," she said, "I think we need to go inside and tell Mommy."

"Do you really think so, Sissy?" Adam asked. "We're having fun out here, and they're not doing anything."

"I know," Cassidy replied. "But you know that Mommy tells us that when she's not with us, we still need to make wise decisions, and I think the wise decision is to go inside. We don't know those people, and we don't know what they're doing, so I think we need to go." She jumped down off of the trampoline and started toward the house, Adam following at her heels. When they reached the house, Cass turned around, and

sure enough, the car was still there.

"Mommy?" she called. "Yes, Honey?" her mom answered from the bedroom. Cassidy and Adam explained the situation to their mom and she went to look out the window. "It has out-of-state license plates, kids, and I think the man inside is looking at a map. They are probably from out of town and just don't know how to get where they are trying to go. I want to tell you, though, that I am very proud of you for coming inside to tell me right away! That shows that you are learning to be decisive, and to make wise decisions. Good job! And now, I'm going to make some brownies to bring to your grandparents' house tonight; do you want to help?"

"Yes!" they both responded instantly. "See, we are decisive, Mommy!" Adam grinned.

DECISIVENESS

IN YOUR LIFE

Questions

1. Your family is at the playground. Your baby sister is crawling furiously towards the spinning merry-go-round. Mom is busy talking. How can you demonstrate decisiveness?
2. At family night at church, everyone is hesitant to be the first to quote a Bible verse. How can you encourage others by being decisive?
3. Your aunt asks you and your brothers and sisters which kind of ice cream you want. Everyone says, "I don't care." How can you respond with decisiveness?

Practical Projects

1. Arrange a situation where you can allow your child to choose between two options. Reward them for being decisive.
2. Read the account of Nehemiah in rebuilding the wall. Point out his decisiveness and how God rewarded the entire nation because of his decisiveness. Point out distractions that came up and how he persisted in accomplishing what he set out to do.
3. Make up some "If's" related to opportunities in your child's life where he can respond with decisiveness.

ENDURANCE

THE INWARD STRENGTH TO ENDURE TRIBULATION WITH DETERMINATION

"For what glory is it, if, when ye be buffeted for your faults, ye shall take it patiently? but if, when ye do well, and suffer for it, ye take it patiently, this is acceptable with God.
For even hereunto were ye called: because Christ also suffered for us, leaving us an example, that ye should follow his steps." −1 Peter 2:20-21

"Let your moderation be known unto all men. The Lord is at hand." −Philippians 4:5

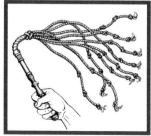

ENDURANCE

IN THE BIBLE

Peter and John before the Sanhedrin

Peter and John were healing many people and were preaching that the power of healing belonged to Jesus Christ, the risen Son of God. The council of religious leaders, many of whom had condemned Jesus also, were extremely irritated by Peter's and John's preaching, and by the attention the two disciples were getting from the people.

They tried numerous times to stop Peter and John, but Peter and John insisted that they must obey God before any human authority. Peter and John endured the persecution of the council for a while, until at last the council was furious enough to kill them.

One member of the council, Gamaliel, suggested that Peter and John be left alone. He said that if they were preaching lies, their following would die out soon enough. But if they were preaching the truth, it would be very dangerous for the council to oppose God's will.

So the council agreed to let Peter and John go, instead of killing them. However, they ordered the two disciples to be flogged before releasing them, and the council tried one last time to tell them never again to preach the name of Jesus.

Peter and John had not only endured the flogging and the pressure of the council without complaint, but they even rejoiced that God counted them worthy to suffer for Jesus' sake. And despite opposition, they continued to boldly preach the message that Jesus was the Messiah.

ENDURANCE

IN HISTORY

Daniel Boone and the Wilderness Trail

Daniel Boone was a simple man, a hunter, a father, and a Christian. But he was also much more: he became famous throughout all America for his great work of blazing a trail through woods and mountains to Kentucky.

Back in Daniel Boone's time, the mid-to-late 1700s, there were only thirteen states. Kentucky was not one of them; Kentucky and the rest of the American continent were nothing but wilderness.

Daniel's first trip to Kentucky was with another hunter, to hunt for food and skins. The land was so good that Daniel Boone thought it might make a good place for a settlement. After a few more hunting trips, he went back with his family and 50 other people to settle there. But the Indians that lived there were not happy about this. They wanted to keep Kentucky for themselves. So the Indians captured Daniel Boone's and another settler's sons and killed them to scare Daniel and the settlers away. The Indians' plot worked—the settlers turned back—but it only worked for a little while. They hadn't counted on Daniel's endurance.

Because of the killing of the settlers, a war was started between the state of Virginia and the Indians for the territory of Kentucky. The Indians lost, and were forced to give Kentucky to the white men.

After this, a man named Richard Henderson hired Daniel Boone to make a trail to Kentucky so that people could travel there and settle. This trail was called the Wilderness Road. Daniel Boone and his 30 men endured a lot on this journey. There was always the possibility of getting lost. And there were wild animals in the woods,

Daniel Boone

and Indians that sometimes attacked them. But they continued with their work, until they reached the Kentucky River.

Settlements were founded, and Daniel Boone took his own family to live in Kentucky in 1775. His fame spread throughout the land, and he became the American legend that he is today.

Daniel Boone on the Wilderness Trail

ENDURANCE

IN EVERYDAY LIFE

A Splash in a Pond

Luke and Adam were best buddies. They loved to spend time together, no matter where they were. One day Adam's dad, Tim, took the kids to a farm to play while he helped the farmer with some work. Tim told the boys they could play in the field where the horses were kept, but not to go outside the fence. Luke and Adam didn't mind that a bit; it was a huge field, and included a pond that they could play in. Sometimes they fished in the pond, and sometimes they had contests to see

who could throw a rock the farthest across the pond, or who could make the biggest splash. However, since neither one of them had learned

to swim yet, they never actually got into the water.

This particular day was a rock-throwing-contest kind of day. Luke was older, but Adam had a good arm for throwing, too, so it was a close match. Luke threw in a rock and said, "Adam, I bet you can't make a bigger splash than that!"

"Oh yes, I can!" Adam chuckled. He picked up the biggest rock he could see, and lifting it up as far as he could manage, he threw it down into the water. The rock certainly made a big splash—and was followed a moment later by another

even bigger splash, as Adam, who had lost his balance when he let go of the rock, also tumbled into the pond!

Luke watched in horror as Adam's head went under the water. "Adam! Adam!" he cried. Adam's head bobbed up again. "Grab my hand!" Luke shouted, and reached out as far as he could without losing his balance too.

Adam grabbed for Luke's hand, and for the next few minutes, they both struggled to hold on. The bank at the edge of the pond was very slippery from all the mud, and Luke was having trouble not falling in himself. Adam was trying to keep his head above the water while also trying to work his way up the steep, muddy bank. Finally, exhausted, Adam was able to crawl out, and the two of them sat there, panting.

"Luke," Adam gasped, "Do you remember what my mom was saying before we left this morning?" "Yeah," Luke said. "She said endurance is the inward strength to endure tribulation with determination. But, um, why do you ask?"

"What does 'tribulation' mean?" Adam continued.

"Well, severe affliction. Distressing circumstances. In other words, it's something that's hard or upsetting," responded Luke, whose vocabulary never failed him, no matter what the circumstance.

" 'Cause I'm pretty sure that was tribulation," Adam said, pointing to the pond. Both boys thought for a minute. "I think you're right," Luke agreed. "And that means you definitely showed endurance."

"And so did you!" Adam added. "You were as tired out as I was. If you had given up, I never would have been able to get out of that pond!

Thanks, Luke. You're a great cousin."

Luke smiled, and the two headed up to the barn to tell Adam's dad all about their adventure ... and how they faced it with endurance.

ENDURANCE

IN YOUR LIFE

Questions

1. You just got a new bicycle and are excited to try it. You jump on and promptly fall over. The bike is larger than your old one. You feel like giving up and crying or getting angry. How can you instead demonstrate endurance?

2. You are running a race to help raise support for kids with cancer. You have a half mile left to go, but your legs are hurting and your lungs burning. The kids with cancer get more money for each quarter mile you complete. There is no time limit on how fast you run. How can you practice endurance?

3. You are almost finished with school for the day. The only thing left is reviewing your Bible verses. Mom wouldn't know you hadn't done them and you feel like taking a rest. How can you practice endurance?

Practical Projects

1. Think of something that easily discourages your child. Help him work out specific goals for showing endurance through it.

2. Help your child plan a project (maybe something nice to do for an elderly person or a younger child) and help them to persist in bringing it to completion, working out steps for enduring.

3. Let your child do a project he's been wanting to do, but explain first of all, that he/she must practice endurance and not give up on it if everything doesn't go just right.

Paul, Changing Plans on His Missionary Journey
Acts 16

FLEXIBILITY

CHEERFULLY BEING WILLING TO CHANGE MY PLANS WHEN CIRCUMSTANCES BEYOND MY CONTROL REQUIRE IT

"Be careful for nothing; but in every thing by prayer and supplication with thanksgiving let your requests be made known unto God. And the peace of God, which passeth all understanding, shall keep your hearts and minds through Christ Jesus."

−Philippians 4:6, 7

FLEXIBILITY

IN THE BIBLE

Paul Changes Plans

Paul was a faithful missionary, sharing the Good News of Jesus Christ with Jews and Gentiles across Asia and Europe. He listened to the Lord, and went where God told him to. This meant that he had to be flexible, because sometimes God's plans were not Paul's plans.

Once, Paul and his friend Silas were trying to go to Bithynia to preach, but the Spirit of Jesus didn't let them go there. This was not the first time they had been stopped from going there. Paul probably wondered why he wasn't to go to Bithynia, but he obeyed God nonetheless.

That night, Paul had a dream that showed him why it was a good thing he had been so flexible. There was a Macedonian man standing in his dream, calling him to come to Macedonia to help the Macedonian people.

Paul now knew why God had said not to go to Bithynia: Paul was needed in Macedonia even more. Because Paul was flexible, God was able to speak to him in miraculous ways, and God was able to use him for amazing things.

FLEXIBILITY

IN HISTORY

General Douglas MacArthur

The **Korean War** occurred only a few years following World War II. A man named General Douglas MacArthur had proven himself a very wise and capable military leader in World War II. He was put in charge of the United States troops in Korea.

The United States was on the side of the South Koreans who were fighting against the North, but things were not looking good. The North Koreans were gaining the advantage, and the Communist Chinese were aiding them—until General MacArthur had a brilliant idea, that is.

President Truman had decided after World War II that there would be no amphibious attacks (which means attacks made from the water), but MacArthur urged him to be flexible.

MacArthur planned to attack Inchon, a Korean port, from the sea. He planned to do it by surprise.

This was not the usual way to go about a battle, and almost everyone was opposed to MacArthur's "brash" plan. It seemed to everyone else that an attack on Inchon was nigh impossible. For one thing, there were high sea walls, swift currents, and poor anchorage at that port—not to mention the possibility of deadly mines. For another thing, the Marine Corps had been greatly reduced after World War II, and so new recruits had to be gathered in very quickly in order to make the attack at Inchon. Last (but certainly not least), Inchon was heavily defended by the North Koreans.

Despite all opposi-

General Douglas MacArthur

tion, however, General MacArthur was confident and he managed to get his plan approved. What a good thing he was able to, for it turned out to be a tremendous victory! On September 15, 1950, the attack at Inchon moved forward. Just as MacArthur had expected, the North Koreans were taken totally by surprise. The United States and South Korean troops were able to take back Seoul, the capital of South Korea.

MacArthur's victory at Inchon has been called the greatest victory of modern war, a victory that could not have been won without flexibility.

General MacArthur walking ashore

FLEXIBILITY

IN EVERYDAY LIFE

Cassidy Makes a Choice

Cassidy was the oldest child in her family, having two younger brothers, Adam and James. She was a big help to her mom. She learned early on how to help clean the house, wash the dishes, help with her little brothers, and all those things that, combined, make mothers feel like they need ten hands to accomplish! Even though she was only seven years old, there was a lot she could do to help.

One day, Cassidy decided to get up and get her school work done early. "This way I can do my chores and take care of James for Mom while she teaches Adam, and still have plenty of time to do what I want to do this afternoon," she told herself. Her mom was still getting ready for the day, so while she waited Cass began working on her daily chores. She hummed as she cleaned her bedroom, folded the laundry, and swept the floors.

As she worked, she began to think of what she would use all her free time for that day. "First," she thought, "I'm going to finish that *Little House* book I've been reading.

Then I think I'll work on that necklace I'm making Aunt Grace... and then..."

Just then the phone rang. Her mom answered it, and a few minutes later she came into the living room. "Hey Cass," she said, "Nana just called to see if you wanted to go out to lunch with her today. She is going to be running some errands and she said she'd like to have some company if you want to go along!"

"Ooh, yay!" squealed Cassidy. "I haven't gone out with Nana in a long time! And I've already gotten most of my chores done, so I should be done with everything I have to do before she gets here!" "Perfect!" replied her mom. "I'll let her know."

Cassidy studied hard that morning, trying to finish her school work up as quickly as possible. Nana was going to be there at 11:00, and she wanted to be ready!

After awhile James woke up and Mom went to get him while Cass helped Adam pick out his clothes to wear. The phone rang again, and Mom called, "Can you get that, honey?" "Sure!" she replied, grabbing the phone.

"Hello?" she said. The voice on the other end scared her. "Hey Cass, this is Daddy. Can you put your mom on the phone?"

"Um, sure, Daddy, but what's wrong?" she asked.

"I need to talk to Mom first; she can explain it to you later," he replied. Cass hurried to give the phone to her mom, then waited anx-

iously until their conversation was over. "What's the matter Mom?" she asked.

"Daddy's sick." Her mom replied. "We're going to have to go pick him up at work and take him to the doctor right away."

Cassidy helped get her brothers ready to go, and then went out to the van. All of a sudden, she remembered. "Oh no! I was going to get to go out to lunch with Nana today!" she thought. "Now I'm going to have to miss it!" Cass tried hard not to be disappointed, but she was. She had been looking forward to having special time with her Nana, and going out to lunch was always a treat, too! She quietly reminded her mom, so she could call Nana and explain, and then closed her eyes.

"Dear God," she prayed, "please be with my daddy,

and help him to be all right! And God... I'm really disappointed that I can't go with Nana today... so please help me to have a cheerful attitude and focus on helping my mom instead of just thinking about what I'm missing."

Soon they reached her dad and hurried him off to the doctor. Cassidy and Adam entertained little James, and tried to make him laugh. Finally the doctor came in. "Good news!" the doctor said. "You are simply coming down with a virus, but your body reacted strangely and went into shock. We see this happen every now and then, but it is not very common." He gave their dad some medicine, and the family went home. All that day and most of the next, Daddy lay in bed. Finally, towards the end of the second day, he began to feel better, and they knew that the virus was almost gone.

The next morning, Mom announced, "Daddy is feeling so much better today that he is going back to work!" "Hooray!" cheered Cass. "Thank you God, for healing my daddy!"

"I wanted to tell you, Cass, how very proud I am of you." her mom continued. "I know you were disappointed that you couldn't go with Nana the other day, but you don't even know what a tremendous help you have been to me. I never could have taken proper care of your dad if I hadn't had you to watch the boys for me. Thank you so much for being flexible, even when it was disappointing for you!"

Cass smiled and said, "God helped me. It was hard, but I knew I needed to do what was right and be flexible." Her mom hugged her. "And now, honey," she continued, "I have surprise. Nana is going to take you and Adam to spend the whole day with her and Grandad and all your aunts and uncles! And, because you didn't get to go with her the other day, she is going to take you out to get lunch and then to get ice cream afterwards!"

Cassidy could hardly believe her ears. "Really?" she asked. "Hooray!" Cass hurried to get ready, thinking all the while, "When you do what you know is right, it always pays off. God blesses us when we are willing to be flexible to help others."

FLEXIBILITY

IN YOUR LIFE

Questions

1. Your family was planning to go to the beach for a week's vacation. You hear on the radio that the beach has been evacuated due to a coming hurricane. How can you respond with flexibility?

2. You had been saving a cookie to eat after rest time. As you walk into the kitchen, you see Dad sitting down to eat it with a large glass of milk. How can you show flexibility?

3. You are excited to be using Sculpey clay today. There is just enough for all the children in your family to use. Your cousin unexpectedly comes over because his mother has to go to the doctor. How can you show flexibility?

Practical Projects

1. Make a list of "If's" (situations you know your child will face) and help him/her work out correct responses in advance.

2. Think of people in the Bible who illustrated flexibility (people who had to change plans). Read their stories from the Bible. *Example:* Abraham, Daniel, Jesus.

3. Think of some specific times in the last few
    months when you should have exercised
    flexibility.

The Good Samaritan
Luke 10

GENEROSITY

GIVING UNSELFISHLY
TO THE NEEDS OF OTHERS

"Give to him that asketh thee, and from him that would borrow of thee turn not thou away."
                                        —Matthew 5:42

GENEROSITY

The Good Samaritan

Jesus was asked one day by an expert in religious law what should be done to inherit eternal life; and the answer was that you ought to love the Lord God with all your heart, and to love your neighbor as yourself. But this was not enough to satisfy the expert, so he asked, "Well, who is my neighbor?"

Jesus answered by telling him the following story:

"While a Jewish man was traveling from Jerusalem to Jericho, a band of robbers suddenly attacked him. They took his clothes, beat him up, and then they left him on the roadside. He was so injured and weak that he would surely die, just lying there without help.

"A priest soon came along the same road. When he saw the poor helpless man lying on the side of the road, he did not stop to help; instead, he crossed to the other side of the road, and kept walking.

"A Levite came along afterward and did the same thing. Would no one help this poor man?

"At last, a Samaritan (who was, in those days, a person despised by the Jews) came along the road. When he saw the beaten man on the roadside, he felt sorry for him, and he took care of the man's wounds. Then he put the man on his donkey, and took him to an inn. He asked the innkeeper to get the poor man whatever was needed, and the generous Samaritan paid for everything himself."

Jesus asked the law expert which of the three passersby in the story was the true neighbor to the poor Jew?

The expert answered that it was the man who had shown mercy—the generous Samaritan.

Jesus said, "Yes, now go and do the same."

GENEROSITY

Andrew Carnegie, Philanthropist

Andrew **Carnegie is remembered** as the second-richest man in history. He is remembered for his work in the Industrial Revolution, among other things.

Most of all, though, he is remembered for his generosity.

He wasn't always a rich man, though. It was hard work and ingenuity that earned him all his wealth. He was born the son of a Scottish weaver, someone who makes cloth and doesn't make much money.

When he was 13 years old, his family emigrated to the United States, where he and his father got work in a cotton mill. It was a very tedious job that did not pay well.

Two years later, his uncle got him a job as a telegrapher. This still was very ordinary work at that time. However, young Andrew worked hard, and made a lot of important friends. He was soon promoted to operator.

Another thing that helped Andrew to rise up in the world was his keenness to learn. He was always pushing himself to learn how to do things better and faster. He knew a man who opened his personal library to working boys, and Andrew took advantage of this opportunity to read all he could.

It was not long before Andrew Carnegie had become superintendent of the railroad in Pittsburgh, Pennsylvania. He began investing money with the help of a wise friend. Things turned in his favor because of wise management, the Civil War, and his work in the iron business.

Then, did he keep all of his money for himself to enjoy? He had been poor once, and he had earned it all by his hard work, so nobody would have blamed him. However, he wanted to give a great deal of his money away. He used it to build and help libraries, schools, and

universities, so that other boys like he had been would have the chance to learn. It was his belief that everyone who was rich ought to use his riches to help other people.

Andrew Carnegie, second-richest man in the world, was also one of the most generous.

Carnegie Steel Works

GENEROSITY

Seven Dollars to Spend

For her birthday, Cassidy had received seven dollars from Uncle Nate and Aunt Tina—one for each year of her life! Cassidy's mom had a system for helping her and Adam use their money wisely, so Cassidy knew that some of the money should be given to God at her church, and that it would be a good idea to save some too, so that she could buy something bigger later on.

Cassidy put aside one dollar to put in the offering plate at church on Sunday. She put one dollar in her piggy bank to save, and then tried to decide what to spend the remaining five dollars on. There were a lot of things she could buy! She thought about buying some doll clothes. "But," she reasoned, "I have a lot of those already." She could buy a game of some sort. She liked games. But then she remembered that she had received two new games for her birthday. "I guess I don't need any more of those right now," she thought.

"Maybe I could spend it all on candy!" she giggled to herself. "If I ate that much candy I would be sick!" She thought and thought, and finally she decided she would use some of it to buy a jump rope. Her cousin Anne had one and Cassidy had been hoping to get one as well so they could jump together. The rest of it she thought she would use to buy a new coloring book, and then if she had any left after that, she would save it.

Cassidy thought a lot about her upcoming purchases over the next few days. She was looking forward to going shopping and picking out the most beautiful jump rope she could find!

Sunday came, and Cassidy carefully put her one dollar for the offering in a separate part of her purse so she could easily take it out to put in the offering. It made her happy to be able to give to God's people, knowing that it would help to tell other people about Jesus.

The pastor was out of town that week, so another man from the church preached instead. This man was a missionary to China, and he spoke about how most of the believers in that country did not even have their own Bibles. Many churches there, he said, had only one or two Bibles for the whole congregation to use!

The missionary showed a video of a group of Chinese believers when he brought in a suitcase full of Bibles. All the people on the video began crying as they picked up what was now their very own copy of God's Word. They jumped up and down for joy and kissed the Bibles. Cassidy's eyes filled with tears. "How many people in the world,"

she thought, "did not know about Jesus. And how many knew, but could not study His Word to learn more about Him and about how they should live their lives?"

At the end of the service, the missionary announced that they would be taking up a collection of money to purchase Bibles for China. Each Bible, he said, would cost about five dollars.

Cassidy thought about the money still in her purse. Five dollars. That was a lot of money for her . . . but it could be the answer to the prayer of a Chinese Christian. She thought about the beautiful jump rope she had planned to buy. She decided she had enough coloring books, but . . . she had really wanted that jump rope. Cassidy looked back at the picture on the screen and suddenly, her jump rope didn't seem so important anymore. When the offering plate came her way, Cassidy dropped in her last five bills. "Dear God," she prayed silently, "please use this money to help other people believe in You. And thank you for helping me not to be selfish, but instead to give to the needs of others."

As she left the church that day, Cassidy had a spring in her step and a smile on her face. She couldn't stop thinking about the person who would receive a Bible bought with her money.

The next day Aunt Kelley stopped by Cassidy's house. "I forgot to give you your birthday gift at your party the other night," Kelley said, "so I brought it to you today." Cassidy opened the gift to find the most beautiful jump rope she'd ever seen! Just then she remembered that Jesus had said, "Give and it shall be given unto you." Her smile couldn't get any wider!

GENEROSITY

IN YOUR LIFE

Generosity

1. You've been busy saving your money to buy a brand new bicycle. You finally have enough money saved. You hear of a family down the street whose house burned down last night. They have five children who just lost all their possessions. How could you demonstrate generosity?

2. You received a whole box of chocolates for your birthday. As you are enjoying them, you notice your brother watching you longingly. What would be a generous thing to do?

3. We can be generous with our time or toys as well as money. Think of someone who would be blessed by you investing a little time in them. *Example:* reading stories to my baby brother when Mom is cleaning.

Practical Projects

1. Help your child find either a poor or sick child to prepare a gift for. Let them either make the gift or shop for it.

2. Assign your child a chore to earn money to support a child in a third world country (see www.allowthechildren.org as a possibility).

3. Encourage your child to begin a "hug" ministry at church. Have them select an older person, maybe a widow or widower who would be encouraged by receiving a hug from your child each week. Who knows what a friendship could begin, while at the same time your child is learning to have a heart of service!

**Paul and Silas in Prison
Acts 16**

JOYFULNESS

CHOOSING TO HAVE A GOOD ATTITUDE EVEN WHEN CIRCUMSTANCES ARE TOUGH TO BEAR

"Rejoice in the Lord alway: and again I say, Rejoice."
—Philippians 4:4

JOYFULNESS

IN THE BIBLE

Paul and Silas in Prison

One day, as Paul, Silas, Luke, and other believers were going to the place of prayer, they met a demon-possessed slave girl who told people's fortunes in order to make a lot of money for her masters. She followed the believers and mocked them. This happened for several days, until at last, Paul commanded the demon, in the name of Jesus Christ, to leave her; and it instantly did.

The slave girl's masters were so upset—because this meant that they couldn't make money off of her anymore—that they had Paul and Silas arrested. Paul and Silas were beaten and thrown into an inner prison, with their feet clamped in stocks, to make sure that they wouldn't escape.

Paul and Silas must have been sore and tired, as well as rather angry, because they were Roman citizens, as it was unfair to treat citizens like that without a trial. Nevertheless, they were praying and singing hymns to God as they sat in the jail that night. They were able to do this because they had the joy of the Lord in their hearts.

Suddenly there was an earthquake, the prison doors flew open, and the chains of the prisoners fell off! When the jailer woke up and saw this, he feared that all the prisoners had escaped, and he would be killed for letting them. So he would have taken his own life, but Paul stopped him. Paul told him that all the prisoners were still there.

Because of Paul's and Silas' faithful example of joy and trust in the Lord, the jailer and his family were saved and baptized. The jailer took care of Paul and Silas until the morning. Paul and Silas, and the jailer and his family, all rejoiced that God had turned this bad situation into such a good one.

Then the city officials decided to let Paul and Silas go free, because they really hadn't done any-thing wrong. Moreover, when the officials learned that Paul and Silas were Roman citizens, they apologized to them and begged them to leave the city so that the officials would not get into trouble for their mistake.

Paul and Silas went to the house of Lydia, to encourage her and the other believers. Not even being beaten or imprisoned could take away their joy.

JOYFULNESS

IN HISTORY

Fanny Crosby

Fanny Crosby was six weeks old when she became ill. She got better, but her sickness and poor doctoring left her blind. To most of us, this is a terrible tragedy; to Fanny, however, it was a blessing.

She also was blessed with an incredible talent for writing poetry, which she used to write over 9,000 hymns in her lifetime. She had written her first poem by the time she was eight years old. It was a poem about the joy she found in being blind.

When she was 15 years old, Fanny was sent to the New York Institute for the Blind. She was a student there, and then a teacher, for a total of 23 years. At first, she was allowed to write her poetry there; but then she was told to stop because it was "vain." Thankfully, though, a certain doctor told the school to let her continue writing.

"Here is a poetess," he said. "Give her every possible encouragement. Read the best books to her and teach her the finest that is in poetry. You will hear from this young lady some day."

The doctor's words certainly came true. Even now, Fanny Crosby is one of the first people you think of when you are trying to name hymn writers.

By age 23, Fanny was already being introduced to Congress and presidents. She soon became quite popular. It was not her popularity, though, that caused her to be joyful.

Once, a preacher said to her, "I think it is a great pity that the Master did not give you sight when He showered so many other gifts upon you."

Do you think Fanny Crosby agreed with him? No, she did not!

Instead she replied without hesitation, "Do you know that if at birth I had been able to make one petition, it would have been that

Fanny Crosby

I was born blind? Because when I get to Heaven, the first face that shall ever gladden my sight will be that of my Savior."

JOYFULNESS

IN EVERYDAY LIFE

God's Plan

Lauren was excited. Today was Saturday, the day her Aunt Christa was going to take her to the park for a picnic! From the moment she opened her eyes that morning, this had been all she could think about. In her mind she could see the swings, merry-go-round, monkey bars, and all the other toys her favorite park contained. There was even a big wooden gazebo where they planned to eat their picnic lunch. Oh, it was going to be so much fun!

Lauren sang as she got dressed, and hummed while she brushed her teeth. (She tried to sing, but it was hard to say the words with a toothbrush moving around in her mouth, so she resorted to humming.)

She bounded into the kitchen a few minutes later. "Good morning, Mommy!" she said, before resuming her singing again. "This is the day that the Lord has made!" she sang, "I will rejoice and be glad in it."

Kate smiled and looked down at her daughter. "Good morning Laur," she responded, then teased,

"Why are you so happy today?" Lauren paused in her singing for a moment to reply, "Aunt Chrissy's taking me to the park today for a picnic, remember? I can't wait!"

Lauren helped her mom wash the dishes after breakfast, and then danced off to her bedroom to play. A little while later, she heard her mom calling her name. She poked her head around the corner of her doorway and said, "Yes, Mommy?"

"Come here, please." Her mom said. "I have something to tell you." Lauren joined her mom in the living room. Her mom was looking out the window, so Lauren looked out, too. To her great disappointment, rain was pouring down outside the window. "I'm sorry, Lauren, but I'm afraid you and

Aunt Chrissy will not be able to go for your picnic today." Her mom said. "I just talked to her on the phone, and we are going to plan a time for next week instead. I'm sorry, honey, but it looks like it will probably rain for the rest of the day."

Lauren's eyes filled with tears. She had been looking forward to this day all week long; now that it had finally arrived, all her plans were ruined! She ran to her room, threw herself on her bed and cried.

Her mom came in a few minutes later and sat down on the bed. "Lauren," she said. "I know you are disappointed. You have been looking forward to this all week." Lauren nodded. "However," her mom continued, "do you think the right response is to run away and cry?"

Lauren thought for a minute. "Why not?" she asked.

"Well, only a little while ago you were singing,

'This is the day that the Lord has made. I will rejoice and be glad in it.' But Laur, is this still the day the Lord has made, even though it is raining?"

Lauren looked thoughtful. "Um, yes, I guess so."

"Who created rain, and Who sent it here today?" Kate asked. Lauren hung her head. "God did," she said.

"That's right," Kate said. "So even though it is raining, and you can't do what you had planned, you know that this was God's plan for your day. He knows far better than we do, and His plan is always far better than ours. No matter what happens, we can still choose to rejoice in the day He has made, and trust that He will work it out for our good."

Lauren wiped her eyes and nodded.

"I want to teach you a verse from the Bible that I think may help you remember to have a joyful attitude even in disappointing circumstances," Kate went on. "Philippians 4:4 says, 'Rejoice in the Lord always. Again I will say, rejoice!' Can you say that after me?"

Lauren repeated it several times. "You see," said her mom, "We are to be joyful in every circumstance, for when we do, it brings glory to God and shows that we trust Him to do what is best." Lauren thought for a moment. "OK, Mommy," she said, "Will you pray with me and ask God to help me be joyful?" Of course her mom was glad to do so.

That afternoon, Lauren came to her mom. "Hey

Mommy, remember when we were shopping and you bought me those pink rain boots? Can I wear them outside and splash in some puddles?"

Kate smiled. "Sure honey! I also got you something else last week that I was going to save for your birthday . . . but I think I'll give it to you early. Today is the perfect day for it, after all!" Lauren hurried to put her new boots on while her mom brought the surprise: a beautiful blue umbrella with ruffles on it—and it was just Lauren's size!

"Oh Mommy, thank you! It's so pretty!" Lauren cried. She slipped her jacket on, took the umbrella and ran out to play in the yard and prayed, "Dear God, I know your plan for my days is better than my own; so please help me to trust you and be joyful no matter what!" Then off she ran to splash in the puddles!

JOYFULNESS

IN YOUR LIFE

Questions

1. You've been looking forward to going to the science museum all month long. The day has finally come, but your little brother woke up with the stomach flu, so the trip is postponed. How can you demonstrate joyfulness in this situation? What can you do to help your little brother not feel bad?

2. You've been working on a kite. It is finally ready. You get it up into the air when a big gust of wind comes and snaps the kite in two. How can you show joyfulness?

3. Think of a time when something happened that you thought was VERY bad, but God used it for your good. Purpose to ask God to help you show joyfulness even when rough things happen to you.

4. Joyfulness is different from happiness. Joyfulness is choosing to trust God even when you don't feel happy. Think of something you are not happy about and purpose to treat it joyfully.

Practical Projects

1. Have your child write Philippians 4:4 on special parchment paper, frame, and hang it in a promi-

nent place in your home as a constant reminder of the right way to respond.

2. Read stories of people in Scripture who maintained joyfulness in difficult circumstances.

3. Teach your child the meaning of the acronym "JOY" to remember when tempted to complain:

JESUS OTHERS YOU

King Solomon Designed the Temple of God
1 Kings 5, 6

ORDERLINESS

MANAGING MY LIFE AND BELONGINGS IN ORDER TO REACH MAXIMUM POTENTIAL

"Let all things be done decently and in order."
−1 Corinthians 14:40

ORDERLINESS

King Solomon Builds the Temple

Solomon became the new king of Israel when his father, David, died. David had always dreamed of building a proper temple for the Lord, but the Lord had told him that it was not his job. It was meant to be Solomon's job, and he got to work on it right away, as soon as he became king.

He sent a letter to the king of Tyre, asking that king to send him some beautiful wood with which to build the Temple. Solomon also sent a labor force to Lebanon to quarry large blocks of stone for the Temple's foundation.

Solomon had the Temple constructed, inside and out, as beautifully and as solidly as possible. It was a glorious place! There were carvings and gold trims and rare wood planking; and the furnishings of the Temple—from the pillars and the ash buckets to the altar and the incense burners—were all fashioned of the finest quality in bronze and gold.

All of the work was conducted in an orderly manner, so that nothing would be forgotten. For God had said to Solomon, "As for this Temple you are building, if you do all I have said and obey my commands, then the promise that I made to your father David will come true through you. And I will never abandon my people Israel."

When the Temple was finally finished, the Ark was brought and put into the Most Holy Place in the Temple. Then a thick cloud filled the Temple— the presence of the Lord Himself. Solomon had carried out everything in the order that the Lord had told him to. Because of this, God was pleased with him, and with the Temple he had built.

ORDERLINESS

IN HISTORY

James Madison

Of course you know that the Revolutionary War was the biggest event in American history—in fact, it was the event that made American history.

You also know of the brave men who fought and died for our freedom and our dear land. Perhaps you don't know, though, what happened before and afterwards.

Before the war was fought, the Declaration of Independence was drafted, which declared that the people of the United States of America had rights that no king could take away. After the war the Constitution was drafted, to secure the rights of the people of the United States. Many great men were involved in the writing of these documents and the founding of the new nation. One of them was James Madison.

James Madison was of great help when the newly victorious nation needed to decide on a form of government. There were thirteen states at that time, which had worked together to win the war against Britain. Because there was not much of a union between the states, the government had no way of collecting taxes to pay off the debts from the war. It was clear that a united government was needed, but the people were not willing to have a king over them again.

James Madison saw the need for orderliness in this budding nation of patriots. He helped to organize a convention in 1787 to discuss forms of government. He was the only one at the convention who really had a plan, which was called the Virginia Plan. It was Madison's idea to divide the power of the nation, so that no one man would become too powerful like the king of England was.

The Virginia Plan went into effect, and is still the basis of our government. There are three branches of power: executive, legislative, and judicial.

Because of James Madison's initiative and orderliness, the nation of America, the land of liberty, was able to stand.

James Madison

ORDERLINESS

IN EVERYDAY LIFE

In an Orderly Way

"**H**ooray, Nana's here!" Anne announced as she watched out the window. She jumped down off her perch on the sofa and ran to the door.

"Nana!" she cried excitedly. Patrick joined her. "Nana!" he chimed in. Nana smiled. "Are you two ready to go to the park?" she asked. Anne and Patrick loved to go to the park with their Nana. Today they were going to have a picnic.

"What are we going to have for lunch?" Anne asked. "You'll see," replied Nana, smiling mysteriously. After she had talked to their mom for a few minutes, Nana was ready to go. She buckled them up in her van, and they were off!

"You know something, Nana?" Anne told her. "I was talking to Mom yesterday, and I asked her what it meant to be orderly, because I had heard someone talking about that and I didn't know what it meant. She told me it means managing or organizing all my things so I can get the most done; like when she makes grocery lists so she remembers what she needs to get and can get it more quickly. Well, I've decided that I'm going to be more orderly too!"

"Have you?" Nana asked. "And how are you going to do that, Anne?" "Well," Anne replied, "first of all, I have started to make lists, too. See?" She held up a piece of paper on which she had written all the activities she had planned for that day. Somewhere near the middle was, 'Picnic with Nana.'

"I write it all down so I make sure I get everything done," Anne explained, "and then I cross it off when I've done it! Yesterday I made a list of everything I needed to clean in my bedroom and I cleaned the whole room! And I have a plan for today, too, if it works out!" Anne grinned.

A few minutes later they arrived at the park. Anne and Patrick had so much fun swinging on the swings, riding on the merry-go-round, play-

ing on the sandy beach near the pond, playing on the slide, trying out new tricks on the monkey bars—oh, there were so many fun activities to do!

After they had played for quite some time, Nana asked, "Who is ready for lunch?" "Me!" the children cried together. They gathered in the gazebo where Nana laid out the food she had prepared. "Ooh, yummy!" Anne said. Patrick just grinned.

As they ate, they talked. Nana asked them both if they were excited about their new baby sister Ella, who was to be born any day now. Of course, Patrick didn't really understand what it meant to have a new baby, as he had never had one before, but Anne understood and was very excited.

"I'm going to help Mom with the baby a lot," she confided. "I'll probably rock her and sing her to sleep sometimes, and help Mom give her baths, and teach her how to smile, and all sorts of things." Nana replied, "That's great, Anne. That will help your mommy out a lot. And maybe you can help take care of Patrick too, while your mom is spending time with baby Ella." Anne nodded as she popped the last bite of her sandwich in her mouth.

"Oh, Nana," she continued, "now is the time for my plan. I'm going to clean up from lunch while you and Patrick go play."

"Oh, Anne, that is so sweet of you!" Nana exclaimed. "Thank you for being a servant!" Anne smiled. "You're welcome!" she said. As Nana walked off with Patrick, Anne began to work, humming softly to herself. She organized everything and carefully put it back in Nana's picnic basket. She put  all the trash in a bag and looked around. The gazebo was neat as a pin. She smiled and called to Nana to come see her work.

"Anne!" exclaimed Nana, as she looked inside the picnic basket. "This looks wonderful! It is so organized and neat! You are learning very quickly how to be orderly. Thank you so much!" Anne smiled as Nana gave her a hug and then ran off to play. "It feels good to do things in an orderly way," she thought. "And it helps other people, too!"

ORDERLINESS

IN YOUR LIFE

Questions

1. Mom is making supper. The babies have toys strewn all over the living room. How could you demonstrate orderliness?

2. Your room is very messy. Start with one type of task, such as picking up dirty clothes. Then move toward another such as putting away clean clothes, then picking up blocks, matchbox cars, dollhouse, etc until it is all done. You will have demonstrated orderliness.

3. You notice your little brother can never find his church shoes. What could you do to help him be more orderly with his shoes?

Practical Projects

1. Help you child to find a "place" for all his possessions. Let him take pictures of different types of toys or draw them and tape pictures to the appropriate containers. *Example:* Dollhouse people, matchbox cars, farm animals, blocks, etc.

2. Write down a plan for picking up their room. *Example:* Start with one type of item—pick up dirty clothes, put away clean clothes, pick up all cars, pick up all people, etc., breaking big projects

into smaller, attainable tasks. Consider making a checklist chart to help them.

3. "Drawer check"

    We would periodically do this with our kids. We would tell them that sometime during the week, I would be checking their drawers to make sure clothes were neatly folded. If they passed inspection, I would leave a treat on their dresser, a box of raisins or bag of M&M's. If done consistently, it really helps motivate them to establish orderly habits.

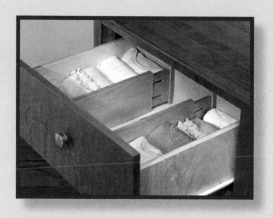

**King Josiah Destroyed Pagan Idols
to Fulfill God's Instructions
II Kings 22 or II Chronicles 34**

THOROUGHNESS

BRINGING TO COMPLETION
EACH TASK I'M ASSIGNED TO
WHILE STRIVING FOR EXCELLENCE

"Better is the end of a thing than the beginning thereof: and the patient in spirit is better than the proud in spirit."

—Ecclesiastes 7:8

THOROUGHNESS

IN THE BIBLE

King Josiah Destroys the Idols

Josiah was eight years old when he became king of Judah. He feared God and followed the righteous ways of his ancestor, King David.

When Josiah was 18 years old, the high priest Hilkiah stumbled upon the Book of the Law in the Temple of the Lord. This wonderful news was taken to Josiah, and Josiah had his secretary read the Book of the Law to him right away.

When Josiah heard what was in the law, he was very sorrowful, because he and his people were disobeying the law in terrible ways. He inquired of the Lord what he ought to do, and the Lord spoke to him through a prophet. The Lord saw his repentant heart and decided to spare Josiah the awful judgment He would have sent.

Josiah gathered all the people of Judah together, from greatest to least, and read the entire Book of the Law to them. Then he promised the Lord that he would keep all of His commands, law, and decrees with all his heart and soul. The people did the same.

Young as he was, Josiah knew that mere words and promises were not enough: true obedience requires action. So he went out and had all of the pagan idols burned. He executed all of the heathen priests who had been leading the people to worship the false gods Baal and Asherah, and even the sun, moon, and stars. The young king removed all of the pillars and shrines, burned them, and ground their ashes into dust.

He also got rid of the witches and fortune tellers in the land, the personal household idols of the people, and everything of the sort. Josiah left nothing undone; he thoroughly destroyed every last trace of idolatry from the land of Judah. He did this so faithfully because it was the Lord's command.

When he was done he returned to Jerusalem, and led the people in celebrating the Passover— the feast that remembers the time God led the Israelites out of Egypt—for the first time since the days of the judges.

It has been said, "Never before had there been a king like Josiah, who turned to the Lord with all his heart and soul and strength, obeying all the laws of Moses. And there has never been a king like him since."

THOROUGHNESS

IN HISTORY

Dr. William Gorgas Drains the Panama Canal

William Gorgas spent his life working to fight a disease called "yellow fever," which a person usually gets from mosquitoes. Perhaps he was so determined because he had gotten yellow fever himself when he was a young man. After he recovered, he dedicated himself to getting rid of yellow fever and malaria altogether.

In William's time, however, most people did not believe that mosquitoes gave people yellow fever. They thought it was a silly idea. But William knew that it was true because of studies done by other wise doctors. He was later proven to be right.

His work took place in Florida, Cuba, and the Panama Canal, where the yellow fever and malaria were the worst. He had several good ways for keeping mosquitoes away, and even killing them. One way that is still commonly used today is putting up mosquito netting. Another method that we still use is fumigation, spraying chemicals to scare off or destroy the pests.

William Gorgas was determined to be entirely thorough in getting rid of the disease-carrying insects: he even drained swamps and ponds, where mosquitoes like to live, so the mosquitoes couldn't live there anymore.

The French had tried to build a Panama Canal once before, but they had not been able to because the yellow fever was so bad. It killed too many of their workers.

Now it was the United States' turn to build a canal, and they had thorough William Gorgas on their side. William Gorgas drained the Panama Canal completely to exterminate the yellow fever plague. Because of his thoroughness, the American workers did not get so sick, and were able to pull through and complete the Panama Canal project.

Dr. William C. Gorgas

THOROUGHNESS

IN EVERYDAY LIFE

Good Work!

"**C**ome here, Luke!" Melody called. They were helping their dad move some wood from a tree they had recently had cut down in their front yard. Uncle Matt had come over, and they were loading the wood into his truck so he could split it up for firewood.

Luke came around the corner of the house. "What do you want, Mel?" he asked.

"Can you help me move this log? It's really big." Mel's small hands and Luke's slightly bigger ones wrapped around the log as they both pulled with all their might. They got it almost all the way to the truck when their dad came over. "Here kiddos, let me help you with that," he said and helped them lift

it into the truck.

Mel went back to the pile and again began picking up branches. While she worked, she made up games, pretending that she was an Israelite slave and had to carry the straw to make bricks. Then she played she was a pioneer girl helping her mother get wood to start a fire. Luke got tired of hauling branches after a while and went off to find something else to do, but Mel kept on working.

"Hey Mel!" she heard Luke call from the back yard.

"Yes?" Mel replied.

"Will you come play with me? I want to have a contest to see who can swing higher on the swings!"

Mel thought for a minute. That sounded like fun. But then she looked back at the pile of wood and knew that her dad could really use her help. She liked to help her daddy, and she wanted to be thorough and complete the job. "In a little while, Luke," she said. "I'm helping Daddy right now."

By now, Melody was

beginning to get tired. After all, she was still a little girl. But she was determined that she was going to keep working and help do a thorough job. Finally all the big pieces of wood had been hauled over and loaded into the truck.

Uncle Matt and Daddy were talking, and Mel started to go inside. Then she looked back and saw three more small branches that had somehow been missed. She looked back at the house, then looked back at the branches. She turned back, picked up the branches, and carried them carefully over to Uncle Matt's truck.

"Thank you so much for your help, Mel!" her dad said. "You've done great!" "Yeah, you did a very thorough job, Mel. Good work!" Uncle Matt agreed. Mel smiled. She wiped the bark off her hands and went inside to take a rest. It felt good to be done, but it felt even better knowing that she had done a

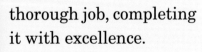

thorough job, completing it with excellence.

THOROUGHNESS

IN YOUR LIFE

Questions

1. Your job today is to clean the baseboards. There is some extra dirt in the corners. How can you show thoroughness?

2. Your dog is shedding. Mom told you to brush her. How can you demonstrate thoroughness in this job?

3. Dad tells you to pick out the rotten apples from the bushel in the basement. How can you, and why should you, do this thoroughly? What will likely happen if you're not thorough?

Practical Projects

1. Make a game out of finding projects not done thoroughly and bringing them to completion.

2. Think of projects that would have negative consequences by not being done thoroughly. *Examples:*
   - fishing, but not preparing the fish
   - picking vegetables from the garden but not picking it all—corn gets tough
   - not wiping the countertops thoroughly and it attracts ants
   - not brushing teeth thoroughly—get cavities

3. Think of people in Scripture who displayed the quality of thoroughness. Read the story and draw insights from it.

RESOURCE MATERIALS

FROM THE LEARNING PARENT

Additional Character Concepts Curriculum Resources
PRESCHOOL

Character Concepts for Preschoolers
• Basic Curriculum

The most important thing you can teach your preschooler is character. *Character Concepts for Preschoolers* provides 36 weeks of lessons for preschoolers, teaching them, first and foremost, character and Scripture, which lays the foundation for all other learning. This curriculum teaches children the meaning of 12 character qualities, and guides them in using wisdom to apply them in everyday life. They are also

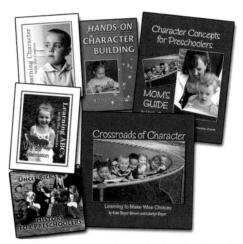

given an appropriate Scripture to learn, so they can find out what God has to say about this character quality.This curriculum will guide you in implementing practical projects to help your child internalize what he is learning. *Hands-on Character Building* is one of the tools we provide, along with instructions for when and how to use it. Your child will learn his ABC's with the colorful *Learning ABC's with the Cousins* flashcards.

Also included in this curriculum are craft and nature projects, season-appropriate where applicable. There are suggestions for science units, and recipes are given to make with your child. Suggestions are made for a field trip destination in coordination with what they've been learning. It is very adaptable to your schedule and is appropriate for use with older children as well.

Resources can be purchased at www.thelearningparent.com

Character Concepts for Preschoolers
• Complete Curriculum

This set includes our brand new *Character Concepts for Preschoolers* Curriculum along with the *Character Concepts for Preschoolers Recommended Resource Pack*—12 items in all.

Additional Character Concepts Curriculum Resources
Ages 6–13

Kids of Character Bible Study

This practical study for children is third in the series of our Character Concepts Curriculum. It teaches 45 character qualites I taught my children, learning what God`s Word has to say about each one and how to apply it to their lives. An added feature contained in this study is **"Ifs,"** a game we often played to help children learn to make wise decisions before they are even placed in a position of temptation. Our grown kids have testified this helped them many times to choose the right thing from having played a game based on insights gained from God`s Word.

Kids of Character Flashcards: This set of flashcards includes 45 character qualities for your child to learn. The definition is provided, as a child has no basis for learning honesty or sensitivity if he doesn't know what it means. Also provided is a Scripture verse for each and instructions for use. Recommended for children ages 6-12, although whatever we learn, we usually do with the entire family!

NEW and IMPROVED LOOK: We have added a table of contents to the study and a picture for each quality! The flashcards now have pictures as well!

Growing in Wisdom Character Studies

This study is based on the popular hand-out *Identifying and Dealing with Offenses* by Marilyn Boyer. Your child will learn 32 types of negative behavior and their Biblical consequences. Through insights learned from God's Word, your child will be guided in making an intentional decision to choose positive, godly character in their day to day life. God has the answer for turning our negative natural tendencies into choices which reflect the character of Jesus Christ.

Growing in Wisdom Flashcards is a set of 32 flashcards to be used in coordination with *Growing in Wisdom Character Studies.* 32 flashcards are provided to help children learn the positive quality that is the opposite of the negative trait demonstrated. On the back side of the card is the Scripture verse which addresses the problem, with its reference and also an insight to be gleaned from Scripture directed at helping your child to make a wise practical decision. Appropriate for ages 7-14. 201 pages.

Proverbs People Collection

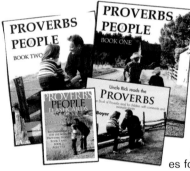

Proverbs People Collection features *Proverbs People* workbooks I and II, our most popular products for children aged seven to twelve. Your 7–12 year olds will learn how to relate to people God's way as they study major character types in the book of Wisdom in practical detail.

In addition, it includes *Proverbs People* flashcards providing two Bible verses for each character type presented in the *Proverbs People* workbooks. The collection also features the 5-cd set, *Uncle Rick Reads the Proverbs.* Pop one of these cd's in at naptime, bedtime, or travel time and your children will hear Uncle Rick read and explain the entire book of Proverbs. They will memorize God's word effortlessly and can go to sleep each night meditating on its mighty truth. Help your child experience the power of Scripture through character study and reinforced listening as well!

Teach your 7–12 year olds how to relate to people God's way! In these two big workbooks, every major character type in the book of Wisdom is studied in practical detail. Teach social and spiritual skills to your child by precept, not by chance!

166

Living the Fruitful Life Bible Study

by Marilyn Boyer

A Bible study course for junior high school students based on how to apply the fruit of the spirit to their lives and the blessings of doing so. *Fruit of the Spirit* **Flashcard Set:** Included are 80 flashcards for memorization and application to daily life.

Words of Wisdom Bible Study

by Marilyn Boyer

Words of Wisdom Bible Study will help your student learn how to use a concordance to dig out insights about the crucial topic of the use of our words and their consequences.

Words of My Mouth **Flashcards** used with the study provides key passages for memorization, meditation, and implementation into daily life.

Power in Proverbs Collection

by Marilyn Boyer

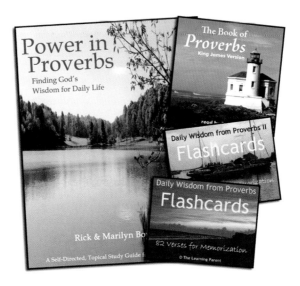

This collection includes Power in Proverbs Concordance Study, two sets of practically applied flashcards–*Daily Wisdom from Proverbs* Sets 1 and 2, and the *Book of Proverbs* CD set. Appropriate for high schoolers.

Power in Proverbs: An exciting new self-study guide to help your teenager take advantage of the matchless wisdom contained in the book of Proverbs! This study teaches your teen how to use the concordance and his Bible to search the Scripture on topics applicable to everyday life.

www.thelearningparent.com